The Best
Stories For Kids

MW01232367

Make Your Kids Daydream Before Bed
With Our Bedtime Stories To Help
Them Get To Sleep

Benjamin Smith

TABLE OF CONTENTS

INTRODUCTION 8

The Unicorn and the Grinning Ghost 10

The Prince and the Unicorn 22

Miley the Naughty Unicorn 32

Harvey the Unicorn......................... 42

Martina the Unicorn 50

Two Unicorns 60

The Unicorn and her Special Day 72

The Unicorn and the Sad Child........ 80

Brindle and the Blue Unicorn 85

The Unicorn and the Eagle 92

The Unicorn and the Spider 98

CONCLUSION 104

INTRODUCTION

Thank you very much for purchasing this book. I wrote these stories to help you and your child have meaningful discussions and to make it easier for your child to understand situations and how others might feel. If we can increase the amount of empathy a child has, that child will be more aware and their relationships with others will improve.

This world needs all the awareness we can give it, so please take some time after reading a story to stop and reflect on the story and the choices the characters have made with your child. Really listen to what they have to say and their feelings and how they would make choices, maybe the same, maybe different.

Enjoy.

The Unicorn and the Grinning Ghost

A smoky mist started to swirl around Brindle and her two new monster friends. Brindle felt very cold. And to be honest, that thought about being afraid of monsters crept back into Brindle's mind.

Brindle was nervous, but when she looked to her new friends, they were just talking between themselves as though nothing was happening.

The mist and smoke got thicker.

Brindle felt a little scared again. This was something new, and she did not think that her new friends were aware of what was happening. Then Brindle had a thought.

What if I just calmly ask my new friends what is happening?

"Um, Savvy and Zesty, is this cold, scary mist normal?"

"Oh, that is just the ghost," said Zombie.

This did not help with Brindle's fear. She was afraid of ghosts. They were all misty and had no body to speak of. They could just pass right through her.

The thought was terrifying.

"I am afraid again, I think," Brindle said.

When her two new friends finally realized that Brindle was in a place of being afraid again, it was too late.

The most horrifying grin appeared in front of Brindle's face. It had ugly pointed teeth that looked like they could tear through anything. And it looked like they had not been brushed in years.

Brindle froze.

"Someone new," said the mouth without the smile, leaving the sharp teeth.

"Hi, Ghost," said Skeleton and Zombie together. "This is our new friend, Brindle."

This casual greeting did not help Brindle with what she saw. It was just a grinning mouth. It seemed very alarming, and all Brindle wanted to do was to make it stop!

"Help?" said Brindle. "Those teeth are mean looking. Please don't bite me!"

With that, the teeth disappeared. And then, over in the corner, the ghost started to appear. It was hunched over in a sad way. It looked down at the ground, but it was still grinning.

Brindle felt emotions coming from this grinning ghost. It was sadness.

"He is sad," Brindle said.

With this, Brindle's fear went away and she knew it was time to go into learning and help mode. It was time to put aside herself and help someone who was sad.

Brindle walked over to the hunched over ghost, "Why are you sad?"

The ghost was almost crying. "I can't stop grinning. I know my teeth are scary. I don't want them to be. I don't want to scare everyone. I am the Grinning Ghost. I can't stop grinning and I scared you with my teeth. Like I scare everyone. That makes me very sad."

Brindle looked over to the Skeleton and Zombie and realized that they felt the same.

The Ghost kept muttering about how he was always scary even when meeting new people. And that his scary teeth got in the way of making new friends.

Brindle hated it when others were sad, so she thought about it.

"I have an idea if you want some help," Brindle finally said to the Grinning Ghost.

"It would be wonderful if you could!" the Ghost said in a hopeful voice. Brindle could feel how lonely he felt.

"Well..." Brindle said slowly. "I think that your teeth are very scary. I was afraid of them. But I also think that you may need a little confidence. Your teeth make you unique and, in a way, very beautiful. Things that are different can be scary to others. When you hide in a corner because you have those teeth, you are not in a place where you can get what you want. So, let's try something okay?"

"Okay," the Ghost mumbled.

Brindle went on, "Let's pretend you are meeting me again. This time Ghost, begin at a distance further away from me. This time, let's talk at a distance first. You are going to have to take into consideration that others may need a little extra time to understand your grin."

"So, get up and let's try this again. The first thing you said to me was..." Brindle tilted her head, trying to remember. "Oh, that's right... Someone new. Say, 'someone new' again from a distance."

"I can try that," the Ghost said with hope.

The Ghost got up and swirled around. Brindle noticed that no matter what the Ghost did, he never stopped grinning. Now Brindle knew that she was about to make another monster friend. Brindle knew that this would work.

The Ghost went a little bit further away and said through his grin, "Oh, look... Someone new."

"Are you referring to me?" Brindle played along.

"I think so," the Ghost was timid.

"I am new and not a monster. I am a unicorn. It is nice to meet you! I am Brindle."

"Oh! Um... Hi... Um... What do I say now?" the Ghost was at a loss.

"Well, I think that you can start with your name and why you have that name. Then you can say that your teeth sometimes scare people and tell them to tell you if they are afraid," Brindle thought about it. "Try that."

"Okay," the Ghost started to talk. "I am the Grinning Ghost. I always grin. I know my grin can sometimes scare people. If my smile makes you uncomfortable, please let me know!"

"That was excellent! Well done!" Brindle replied. "Now I will tell you how I will reply to that."

Brindle paused. "Can I see your teeth?"

The Ghost had never been asked this question before. Even while still grinning, Brindle could tell that the ghost did not know what to do. Then Brindle thought she saw the ghost shrug, and sure enough... It wandered over.

"Okay..." said the Ghost "No one has ever really looked at my teeth before. Go ahead."

Brindle examined those sharp, scary grinning teeth. "Yes, they are extremely scary!"

But Brindle found herself not so scared. She became very curious.

"Do you have to grin all the time?" she asked.

"Yes," the Ghost replied through his scary teeth.

"Hmmm... I see. Well, my friends are accepted for who they are, no matter what they look like. I think we are friends now. What do you think?" Brindle asked.

"I have never been friends with anyone other than other monsters. I would really love to be your friend, Brindle!" the Ghost no longer seemed sad.

"Then we are friends now!" Brindle announced. "And I accept you for everything you are... including those sharp, terrifying teeth."

Brindle did not know whether telling Ghost its teeth were sharp and terrifying would help or hurt.

"My teeth are indeed sharp and terrifying," Ghost replied. "Since you accept them, Brindle, I will accept them too."

And with that acceptance of how someone looks, no matter how they look, Brindle now had a third monster friend.

The Prince and the Unicorn

Prince Alexander coughed out sea water, stumbling on the sand. He wiped his face off, and looked around. This beach was unfamiliar, and the trees rose up high into the sky. The prince stared at the open ocean in front of him, searching for his ship. It was nowhere to be seen. Alexander sighed. He closed his eyes, remembering the storm. How the thunder crashed and boomed all around them. The waves, taller than some of the towers back home, stretching high above the sails and crashing down on the ship. It was only a peaceful mission at sea, visiting the other Five Seas Kingdoms, with his parents. They were on their way to the final kingdom, where Princess Grace was waiting. He could hear his father calling out his name to come below, but the final wave had crashed onto the ship, pulling Alexander out into the open sea.

The prince punched the sand angrily. He should've listened to his father and gone down below decks, safe from the towering waves.

But he didn't. He chose to stay outside, and watch the chaos rain down on the ship, help where he could, and have some fun. Alexander sighed, staring out at the blue waters that stretched endlessly past the horizon. A few waves broke at the beach he was stranded on, the tide washing in over his boots. Well, boot. One must've gone missing when he was swept out to see. Standing up, Alexander decided now wasn't the time to mope. He had to figure out where he was and how to get to either home or one of the five kingdoms. The prince brushed sand out of his curly brown hair, and walked toward the trees.

He pushed aside branches, following a worn-down path through the forest. The sound of rushing water greeted his ears, and Alexander rushed to the sound. He didn't realize how thirsty he was until he heard the sound of water. He burst through the big green leaves, spotting a huge waterfall pouring into a lake. Scrambling toward the water, Alexander dunk his head inside the waterfall, and drank as much water as he could. When he finally got his fill, he paused, seeing something out of the corner of his eye. A large blue unicorn dipped its head peacefully on the other side of the lake, drinking some of its own water.

Nervously, Alexander backed away from the waterfall, slipping on some of the rocks.

He fell backward into the water, landing on his bottom with a loud splash. The unicorn looked up, staring in his direction. It blinked slowly, snorted, and returned to its drink. Alexander sighed in relief. As he moved to climb out of the water, he heard some giggling behind him. The prince spun around, slipping once again on some rocks. A young girl with long, braided blue hair was sitting in the sunlight on a few dry boulders, as if she was just drying off. She wore a small yellow top, with a lighter blue skirt. "Hi there," she said, sitting up.

"How long have you been sitting there?" Alexander asked nervously. He wondered if she saw his fall, or worse, saw him come in from the jungle like a crazy person.

"Long enough!" the girl said, with a smile. "You look lost."

"I think I am lost," he answered. "Do you know where I am?"

"Well, I think you've found yourself in my home. This lake belongs to me." The unicorn on the other side of the lake whinnied loudly, and the girl waved her hand. "And sometimes Xavier. But he owns all the islands around here." The girl jumped off the rocks and into the water. Her legs were gone, replaced with a blue mermaid tail instead, swimming right back over to Alexander. "My name is Lyn."

Alexander blinked, staring at the mermaid. This was it. He was dead. Mermaids couldn't be real. But he introduced himself anyways, only as Alexander. "Is there any way off this island?" he asked. "I have to get back to my ship. Or the Fifth Kingdom. That's where we were heading anyway."

Lyn looked at Alexander, her bright blue eyes pouring into his. She smiled, and Alexander blushed slightly. She was a beautiful mermaid, but he shook his head. Grace was still waiting for him. The mermaid laughed. She said. "Maybe Xavier can take you!"

Xavier the unicorn looked up. He entered the lake, swimming over to Alexander with ease. He paused by the prince, looking him up and down. Alexander had never been this close to a unicorn before. The creature was a lot bigger than a normal horse, and his horn sparkled in the sunlight. The unicorn tapped him with his horn, and snorted again, stamping his foot. He glanced at the mermaid for a quick moment, then back to Alexander.

"Xavier says he can take you. He trusts you will make a wonderful king someday, and only asks that you keep these islands a secret," Lyn said. "That's a shame, really. I was kind of hoping you could stay here!" She jumped backwards, swimming below the lake surface. The mermaid returned with a sparkly blue stone. "Please give this to Princess Grace. She'll understand." She smiled sadly. "Oh, one more thing." Lyn pushed herself on the rocks, and kissed him on the cheek. The mermaid giggled, and disappeared beneath the lake. She swam far enough away and called out, "Goodbye, Prince Alexander!"

Alexander blushed again. He waved goodbye and turned to the unicorn, who knelt down, waiting for him to climb on. "Thank you," he said as he climbed on. Xavier whinnied, and took off, charging to the island beach.

He galloped as fast as he could across the ocean waters. The blue sea seemed to fly by as they crossed the water, until finally, he stopped just outside the Fifth Kingdom. Xavier snorted, and lowered his head. "I got it," Alexander said. "I can swim from here." He slipped off the unicorns back and into the cold ocean water. As the prince swam away, he glanced back at the water where the unicorn stood. He waved goodbye once more, and swam to the shore, Lyn's kiss still on his mind. Alexander kept swimming, until finally, he made it to the shore, exhausted.

Shouts rang out from the castle, and just before he closed his eyes, he saw Grace, his mother, and dozens of others racing toward him with shouts of relief.

Miley the Naughty Unicorn

This story is about a girl, a unicorn girl called Miley. Miley had a little brother called Bo. Bo, the unicorn, was awesome; Bo was kind, sweet, and was never in trouble. Bo never did anything wrong, and as far as Miley was concerned, Bo was his parents' favorite. He was good at magic, flying, and he was even good at math. Bo made Miley very mad.

Miley, on the other hand, was her own special and sweet self, but she always seemed to be in trouble, and she wasn't good at math.

"But you don't have to be good at math to be a good person," she thought.

She tried to be good, she tried to do exactly what her brother Bo did, but sometimes she'd say something wrong, she'd do something at the wrong time, or it wasn't the right moment talk. Something was always wrong.

Because of that, poor Miley, the unicorn, decided that the only way she seemed to get attention was if she was bad. Because there's no point in her being good because of her perfect brother. Her mom and dad noticed her even though she was bad, and it wasn't good attention, it was bad attention.

Miley was stuck in this loop, where she always behaved badly and got bad attention. Everybody just assumed she was bad, so she had to behave badly and then everybody just said:

"Oh, Miley's always in trouble."

"Miley's not a good girl."

"Miley's always bad."

"Miley always does everything wrong."

It didn't take very long before that became exactly what Miley was. She couldn't get out of the cycle, and now she's known as Miley the bad one, whereas Bo was the good one. Miley's always in trouble; Bo is just a dream to be around.

Miley didn't want to be bad; she wanted to be good like her brother. She wanted to be seen, she wanted to be loved, and she wanted her mum and dad to love her just as much as they loved her brother. What Miley didn't realize was her mum and dad loved her just as much as they loved Bo.

Miley was good at so many things, but she'd found herself in this trap where all she ever did was the wrong thing. Miley was artistic, and she had a wonderful voice, but she hardly ever sang, and she hardly ever drew or painted or created stuff. She seemed just to get stuck in being the bad unicorn.

How many bad unicorns do you know? Not many. Most unicorns are good just like Bo with magic and rainbows and all the wonderful stuff. You never hear about a bad unicorn. So the fact that Miley would get in trouble made it even more dramatic in the unicorn community.

"How dare we have a bad unicorn?"

"What shall we do with this naughty unicorn?"

"She's so naughty," they would all say to themselves.

Miley just wanted some love. She wanted to be seen, loved, and appreciated; she didn't want to be bad.

Miley decided one day that maybe if she did something good in the community, she could climb out of this hole that she got herself in. Even though she was angry at her parents, angry at everybody in the community, and angry at her brother, she decided that there was no point in being angry. It wasn't getting her anywhere, and she was tired of negative attention.

One night at dinner, Miley suggested to her parents that it might be a good idea if the whole community come together to have some kind of art competition. Her parents thought it was a very good idea.

After a couple of weeks of organizing the art competition, one weekend, on a bright sunny Saturday, everyone came out of their homes and brought out their projects. The talents, knowledge, drawings, whatever it was.

One by one, each one of them did something unique.

Even if they all sang, each one of them sounded unique, not one single unicorn was the same.

Miley sang in front of all of the community. When she finished, everyone clapped their hooves. Miley didn't know what to do with herself; she felt warm and fuzzy inside and embarrassed. She was embarrassed that everyone was clapping for her but also at the same time it was so nice.

So nice to not be in trouble; it was so nice to be seen as Miley the singing unicorn instead of Miley the naughty unicorn, the troublesome unicorn.

Miley was getting positive attention for something that she was good at, and this made her feel better about herself. Because she felt better about herself and she wasn't angry anymore, she didn't feel the need to be naughty anymore.

From that day forward, sometimes she would make mistakes, and sometimes she would still get into trouble, but it got less and less and less. Miley became more and more who she wanted to be.

The most important thing was that her mum, dad, her brother, and herself were not stuck in that awful loop anymore. She didn't have to carry on being naughty. Her brother didn't have to carry on just being the perfect one.

The more that she became more normal, less angry, and less naughty, the more she noticed her brother also made mistakes, also had problems and also needed love and attention from their mum and dad. He wasn't so perfect, after all.

If this story sounds like you, whether you're Miley or Bo, how about you try something different? Maybe everything will stay the same, but if you keep trying, things may eventually change. Things will eventually get better.

You don't have to be the same person, stuck in the same old ways. You can change things right now in your mind so that when you wake up tomorrow, it will be a whole new day, a whole new world just like Miley.

Harvey the Unicorn

Caitlyn was a very lucky little girl; her mummy and her sister bought her a horse. The horse's name was Harvey. He was a very handsome horse, very kind and sweet and loving. Caitlyn loved Harvey. What Caitlyn's mom and sister didn't know was that Harvey wasn't just an ordinary horse. Harvey, in fact, had a secret, a secret that only Caitlyn knew about - Harvey was a unicorn.

That's right; he wasn't just an ordinary horse. In the day and to everyone else, he looked like Harvey, the ordinary horse. He was kind, sweet, and loving, but that's about it; there wasn't anything special about how he looked.

He didn't have a unicorn horn, he wasn't rainbow-colored, and he didn't have sparkles coming out of his ears, so no one suspected the truth.

But the truth that was when the sun went down at the end of the day, and the moon came up, and the stars came out in the sky, Harvey became a unicorn.

One of the most favorite things in the world for Caitlyn is to climb on Harvey's back when the rest of the world was asleep and fly; fly high in the sky with Harvey.

She would wait till the whole house went quiet, then she'll go downstairs, go out back to the barn, rub Harvey's nose and give him a kiss in the center of his forehead and all of a sudden the magic would happen.

There would be lightning, sparkles, balloons, rainbows, and bells, and then Harvey would be standing there a unicorn.

She would climb up on his back and say:

"Let's go somewhere special tonight. Take me somewhere special, Harvey."

And Harvey would say

"Hold on tight, Caitlyn. Are you ready?"

He would move his hooves on the ground as if he was preparing himself, and then all of a sudden, they would be up over the barn, over the trees, and up over all the houses around. They keep going up, going higher and higher in one direction. Harvey knew exactly where he would take her tonight.

He would take her to one particular star, a star where only the rock people lived. They were going higher and higher and higher still until it felt like Caitlyn had been flying for the longest time. Going higher and higher up through the clouds up towards the stars, up past the moon even until they got to one particular star.

A star that looked very rocky when they landed on it.

There was no one in sight just bumps all over the earth, rocks, gravel, and hills in the background.

Caitlyn looked at Harvey and asked:

"Why are we here? Where are we?"

Harvey said:

"This is the star where the rock people live; watch."

All of a sudden, Harvey lifted his front hooves and clapped them together three times, and then he placed his hooves back down on the ground. All of the rocks started to move. What looked like big rocks all around her were tiny little rock people.

When the rocks moved and opened up, they were like turtles; they had arms, legs, and heads with big smiley faces, with big smiley eyes.

It turns out that rock people like to hug; they hugged Caitlyn, and they hugged Harvey. They also hugged each other. They pile up into piles of rocks and to everyone else in the world, to everyone else in the universe; it just looks like a star made of rocks, but it isn't. It's a star made of rock people; cutest little rock people ever and they don't talk. They just walk around, go about the day, hug each other, and they look so happy, friendly, and sweet.

"What a cool place," thought Caitlyn.

They stayed at this particular star for a long time until it felt like Caitlyn had hugged all of the rocks individually. They all hugged differently; each one of them had their signature hug. Some hugged tight; some hugged gentle and soft, some of them hugged her and tapped her on the back while they hugged her. She felt like she knew all of the rock people by the time she hugged them. Who would have thought that something as simple as a hug could tell you so much about a person?

After some time, Caitlyn got back on Harvey, and they decided to fly down. They flew down through the stars, down past the moon, back down through the clouds, down to the trees and the houses until eventually, she could spot her own house.

They landed on the ground safely, and then all of a sudden, Caitlyn felt herself turning over in bed.

She opened her eyes a little bit and saw the clock on her bedside table, and it said 2:00 a.m.

She was sleepy, her eyes were heavy, and her body was heavy. She had everything on her mind about Harvey being a unicorn, the rock people, the star, the journey, all of their hugs, how wonderful, cute and sweet they were, all of it was on her mind.

But was it real?

She couldn't tell. She didn't know if it was real or if it was a dream, but she loved the idea of Harvey being a unicorn.

Harvey was definitely a unicorn.

Martina the Unicorn

This story is about one of my friends; she's a secret friend, a friend that you can't tell anyone about, but she is a very special friend. My special friend is called Martina, and she's so pretty.

Martina is a unicorn.

She's no ordinary unicorn, not that unicorns could ever be ordinary. They come in different colors; different sizes and they all have very special magical powers.

Martina was known for the fact that she was the best gymnast you would ever see. Martina had been working, enjoying and playing gymnastics since she was a very little unicorn.

Now she was 12 years old. She was very good at gymnastics; her nickname was "ten out of ten"; that's how good she was at gymnastics.

People would say:

"Hey, it's ten out of ten."

And she just giggles and smiles, but she was honestly super fantastic at gymnastics.

Her favorite thing to do was freestyle on the mat, but she could do all sorts of things. She could do acrobatics, but she was especially very good on the balance beam; she barely ever fell off because she had been doing gymnastics almost all her life, and she was so good.

Whenever she performs, she would do this amazing smile that was bigger than her movement. Sometimes her smile was so wonderful to look at that she made everyone happy. She had big white perfect teeth.

Martina noticed something that was a little bit upsetting. One of her teeth at the front somehow got wiggly, wiggly as if it was about to fall out.

The problem was that Martina was afraid of the dentist. And in the past, whenever she got wiggly teeth, her mom had always taken her to the dentist just to make sure everything was just right, but Martina did not like the dentist; she was frightened.

For some reason, even though her dentist was very nice, it was as if when she got inside the dentist's office, the smell of the dentist and how it looked inside the dentist's office always made her nervous and scared. So the idea of having to go to the dentist for her wiggly tooth was not fun.

She'd been avoiding telling her mom, but when she performed, did her gymnastics and her wonderful smile, sometimes a tooth would wiggle when she smiled. Without even realizing it, she was becoming very conscious of her wiggly tooth.

Martina had a friend called Lily, and Lily was not afraid of the dentist. Lily had sparkly, white, beautiful teeth just like Martina, and Lily loved the dentist.

Lily said to Martina:

"How about I go with you to the dentist's office."

Martina said:

"I'll ask my mom, but I'm sure she'll say it's fine that you come along with me."

She finally built up the courage to tell her mom that she had a wiggly tooth, and it was probably time for the wiggly tooth to come out; it was barely hanging on by a string. It was ready to come out, and Martina's mum agreed that Lily could come too to keep her company.

They were going to the dentist's office on Thursday morning. Thursday morning came around, and Martina had barely slept.

They went to pick up Lily. On the way, Lily started to tell Martina about this wonderful thing she does to help her with the dentist.

"It's a breathing exercise," Lily said, "my mummy taught me when I was small, and I do it every time I go to the dentist."

"I breathe in for the count of three, and I breathe out for the count of three. I count in my head, and I do this the whole time I'm in the dentist's chair. And guess what Martina, it makes me feel calm, safe, and it takes my mind off whatever it is that the dentist is doing even if I have to have a filling."

"I've had fillings in the past," said Lily, "too much candy, not enough tooth brushing, but I wasn't afraid; I was very calm, and I did the breathing exercise all the time, and it works Martina."

Martina said:

"Okay, Lily. I will try the breathing exercise."

Lily said:

"I'll count first until you get used to it."

She said:

"Close your eyes and imagine that you're in a very nice place, your favorite place in the entire world. It could be at the beach, at a funfair, in your mummy's arms, it could be hugging your daddy, riding a horse, and so on."

"Close your eyes," said Lilly, "take a nice, deep breath, and I'll count."

"One, two, three; hold your breath. Breathe out, two, three. Breathe in, two three, breathe out two three. Breathe in two, three, breathe out two, three."

"Do that the whole time Martina, and if the dentist asks you a question, you can still answer the question, but you get straight back into closing your eyes and doing the breathing exercise," Lily concluded.

Of course Lily was right, Martina was calmer, more peaceful and she did exactly what Lily said.

She closed her eyes, and she imagined that she was in a perfect place in the world and she counted one, two three: one, two, and three until she was finished and the dentist said:

"Okay you're completely done Martina, the tooth is out."

"Oh," she said, "I never even felt a thing."

"I noticed that you were counting," said the dentist, "I noticed that your breathing was very smooth, timed and constant. I thought to myself that you must be doing some kind of breathing exercise."

"I was," said Martina.

"It was my idea. I told her to do it, and it worked," said Lily

"Thank you, Lily," said Martina.

The following week, Martina had her gymnastics performance, and she smiled with no wiggly tooth. She smiled so big that probably every single unicorn in the audience watching could see her tooth was missing, but she didn't care.

She did everything perfectly with the biggest, widest, toothy smile in the entire world.

When you go to the dentist or when you are in a stressful situation, try doing what Lily and Martina did. Make sure that you try it, and I bet you that the experience will be so much better.

Two Unicorns

Sarabelle and Talli were playing one day in the Rainbow Woods. The two white unicorns played there often because they loved how colorful the woods were, with each tree being a different color. Everywhere they looked, they saw red trees with leaves of every shade of red, blue trees with leaves of every shade of blue. Green trees with leaves of every shade of green. Purple. Azure. Pink. Yellow. Garnet. Orange. Turquoise. Brown. Magenta. To Sarabelle and Talli, the colors seemed endless and, no matter how long or how far they explored, they never saw two trees that were the same color.

The ground sparkled with pebbles in places and, in others, was covered with grass and flowers of even more colors and varieties. Sometimes the unicorns would lay in the grass and watch the gentle wind ruffle the flowers and the leaves on the trees, and it was like looking at a rainbow flowing across the woods. Other times Sarabelle and Talli would play chase and run after each other as fast as they could, making the passing colors of the trees, grass, and flowers turn into a rainbow blur.

Today, the friends were walking under the trees and watching the butterflies flit and fly from one flower to another, stopping to take a long drink of nectar before moving on to another flower, when Talli heard someone singing a song.

"Do you hear that?" she asked Sarabelle.

"Hear what?" Sarabelle answered.

"I hear someone singing," Tally said, as she stopped and tilted her head, trying to listen and see where the song was coming from.

Sarabelle stopped and listened carefully. At first, she did not hear anything, but then she, too, heard the faint, soft sound of someone singing. "It sounds like it is coming from the stream," she told Talli.

"Let us go to the stream and see who it is," Talli called as she began to walk away towards the stream.

"Talli, I do not know if we should," Sarabelle called after her friend. "I have never seen anyone else in the Rainbow Woods, and we do not know who this might be." But Talli continued to walk away. Sarabelle, not wanting her friend to go alone, ran a little ways to catch up, then the two unicorns continued walking together to the stream that ran through Rainbow Woods.

The singing became clearer and louder as they walked closer and closer to the stream. When they came to the stream, at first, neither unicorn saw anyone there, but they both could still hear the singing.

"Hello?" Talli called out. "Who is there?"

The singing stopped abruptly, and the two unicorns watched as a bright yellow bush began to shake. A moment later, a small mouse crawled out from underneath the bush. Now, Sarabelle and Talli had seen a mouse before, but they had never seen one who looked like this mouse. Instead of being black, brown, gray, or white, the colors of the mice that they had seen in the past, this mouse was every color that they had ever seen. He looked like a small version of the Rainbow Woods, with his stripes of blue, green, red, purple, pink, orange, and every other color. Even his whiskers were different colors. The only thing about him that was not colored was the white bag he had strung crosswise across his body and hanging down next to his hip.

"Hello, there," the mouse called up to the two unicorns, "my name is Pitar. Who are you?"

"I am Talli, and this is Sarabelle," Talli answered back. "We have never seen anyone else in the Rainbow Woods, and we play here all of the time. Where are you from?"

Pitar looked up at Talli and tilted his head to the side. "Well," he began, "there are many creatures who live in the Rainbow Woods, but most are very shy and do not often let others see them."

"Really?" Talli asked. "Who else lives here?"

"Oh, all sorts of creatures.

Mice, for sure, but there are fish that live in the water, turtles, birds, rabbits. Really, most creatures that you would think you would find living in the woods," Pitar answered. "What are you doing in the woods?"

"We like to come here and look at all of the different colors," Sarabelle answered. "At home, the grass is only green, and the trees are brown and green. The flowers are different colors, but not like the ones here."

Talli added, "The Rainbow Woods is our favorite place to walk or just to lay in the grass and look up at the trees. We like imagining what it would be like to not be all white. To have a horn that was a different color or to have hooves that were not white or a mane that was colorful, like you are."

Pitar continued to watch the two unicorns, silent and thinking. "Well," he began, slowly, as if he was unsure about what he was going to say, "I know how you can be different. It is how I am all different colors, and how all of us who live in the Rainbow Woods look like I do."

"Really?" Talli began to feel excited. She had always wanted to look different, to not be completely white from her mane to her hooves. "How?"

"Well, you have to eat Rainbow Root," Pitar told them. "We eat Rainbow Root every day, and it keeps us looking like this."

"What happens if you stop eating it?" Sarabelle asked.

"You go back to looking the way you did before," Pitar answered. "You have to eat Rainbow Root every day to stay like me."

"Could we eat some?" Talli asked, getting more and more excited.

"I only have enough for one," Pitar said. "I was looking for more when you found me. Rainbow Root is not easy to find. That is why some creatures in the woods do not eat it."

"Could I try it?" Talli asked. Pitar reached into his bag and pulled out a root that, to the two of them, looked just like any other root. It was brown, about the size of a small carrot, and had smaller, hairlike roots branching off from it.

"Talli, what about me?" Sarabelle turned to her friend. "He only has enough Rainbow Root for one."

"Yes," Tally began, "but since I was the one who first heard him singing, I should be the one to try it." With that, Talli leaned over and ate the root that Pitar was holding up.

At first, nothing happened. But as Sarabelle watched her friend, she began to see Talli's mane turning different colors, starting at the bottom and spreading to the ends. Looking down, she saw that her friend's hooves were no longer white, but striped with different colors. Before long, Talli looked just like the Rainbow Woods: every color that could be imagined.

Talli walked over to the stream and leaned over the water, trying to see her reflection. "Look at me!" she exclaimed. "I am every color!"

Pitar walked up to her. "You look like you belong in the Rainbow Woods now."

Sarabelle watched the other two and began to feel jealous. She wanted to be different colors, too. "Could you get more Rainbow Root and let me try?" she asked Pitar.

Pitar turned to Sarabelle. "I am sorry, but I need to go home. It is getting late."

"Could we meet you tomorrow?" she asked.

"Yes, could we meet you tomorrow so I can have more, too?" Talli asked.

Pitar looked from one unicorn to the other. "I do not think that is a good idea," he began. "You have to eat Rainbow Root every day, and it is hard to find. I gather enough for my family, and that takes a long time. I do not want to start gathering for the two of you, as well." With that, he turned and quickly scurried off.

"Wait! Stop!" Talli called, but he was too fast and disappeared into the woods.

"Well, even if he will not give me more Rainbow Root, I am colorful now. We should go home so I can show everyone my colors."

Sarabelle stared at her friend. "Why did you take the Rainbow Root when there was only enough for one? You could have given it to me."

"But I wanted it," Talli told her. "And I was the one who heard Pitar singing first."

Upset, and not knowing what to say, Sarabelle turned and began walking home.

- What do you think about Talli's choice to eat the Rainbow Root?
- Was it safe to eat something from someone she had just met? Why or why not?
- Was it selfish to eat it and not give it to Sarabelle? Why or why not?
- How do you think Talli's family will respond when she comes home and is a different color than when she left that morning?
- What do you think will happen to the two unicorns next?

The Unicorn and her Special Day

Brindle was a very special unicorn who loved meeting new people, helping others and learning new things. She was beautiful and white, with a golden horn. Best of all, Brindle was magic!

One day Brindle was walking around, thinking about all of the adventures she had recently had, and all of the new friends she had made. It had been quite the adventure lately!

It was a bright sunny day, and Brindle paused for a moment to feel the warmth of the sun, and feel the fresh breeze in the air. She reached out with the magic of her horn, and she felt... happy! It was strange, but a good feeling. The happy wasn't coming from her, but she could feel a big happy coming from somewhere nearby. Someone was very, very happy. The thought made Brindle smile, and then she laughed with the pure joy of it.

"I love happy!" Brindle said. "Happy is the best thing in the whole world!"

When she opened her eyes, she saw a light flash in the trees. That had to be the will o' wisp. It was fainter right now in the daylight, but she was sure that was him. So, Brindle decided to wander over in his direction.

Just like when she first met him, when she came close to where he was, the light winked off.

"Yay!" Brindle said to herself. "Someone who wants to play! I hope he's keeping true to his word and only taking people to beautiful places."

Brindle saw the light appear again, still faint in the sunlight, but bright enough for her to see.

"Let's play along," Brindle said, and she once again followed the will o' wisp. Brindle was a little excited. "I wonder what beautiful place he is taking me to?"

Brindle followed the will o' wisp through the trees, blinking first in one place and then turning off and blinking in another place, leading Brindle on a new adventure. She could feel the happy feeling growing, getting closer, and she became even more excited.

Finally, the will o' wisp took her to the rock she had met before, on the edge of the trees next to the field of flowers.

"Hello, Mr. Rock," Brindle smiled happily.

"Hello, Brindle!" the rock replied. "It is very nice to see you again."

"I agree!" Brindle said. "Are you friends with the will o' wisp? I think he brought me here to see you. Did you need something?"

"The only thing I need from you, Brindle, is for you to step around to the other side of me," the rock said mysteriously.

"Oh!" Brindle said in surprise. "All right, then that is what I will do."

Brindle stepped around the other side of the rock, on the side with the field of flowers and she was blasted with the feelings of happiness, coming from all around her, and even coming now from her.

Sitting in the field of flowers were almost all of the friends that she had recently met and shared adventures with...

There was Brup... and his frog brother and sister, Brap and Brop... Cal the caterpillar now turned butterfly... Mari the horse...

Benni the beaver... Elli the eagle... Leon the lion... Berri the bear... Sadie the Spider... Fanny the fairy... Toby the troll... the colored unicorns... Red, Blue, Yellow, Green, Purple, and Orange...

Even her monster friends were here... the Zesty Zombie... Savvy Skeleton... Ridiculous Rat... Grinning Ghost... Misunderstood Medusa... Devilish Dragon... and the Sun shined down on top of them all.

There were colors and streamers everywhere, with tables and tables of food and drink of every kind. There was even a big cake with a single candle on top. And the cake had her name on it... it said, Brindle!

"What is all of this?" Brindle said, a little overwhelmed.

"It is your birthday, Brindle!" the Sun said from the sky.

"It is?" Brindle asked. "I didn't know that!"

"It is," the sun said. "I was there, bright and shining in the sky the day that you were born."

"Oh, my!" said Brindle. "Then this is all for me?"

"It is!" all of her friends cried out. "We wanted to show you just how much we love you and are glad to be your friends! You have taught us and helped us so much. We just wanted to show you how special you really are!"

Brindle had never felt so special or happy in her whole life as she went and joined her friends for her party adventure.

The Unicorn and the Sad Child

Brindle the magic unicorn was a happy little adventurer who loved to make new friends and have adventures, learning new things.

One day, Brindle was walking along the edge of a neighborhood and came across a playground where there were all kinds of things for children to play on and have fun. The thought of children like her friend Hannah playing and having fun made Brindle smile.

Then she felt a sadness coming from someone in the playground. Brindle looked around to see if she could find where the sadness was coming from. And she did. Hiding in one of the playground toys was Hannah, her human child creature friend from the beach. But Hannah looked very, very sad.

Brindle poked her head in through the hidey-hole where Hannah had tucked herself away and blew some sparkles from her horn in Hannah's direction. "Why are you so sad, Hannah?"

"Oh, Brindle!" Hannah cried. She stuck her foot out toward Brindle. "I have something stuck to my foot and I can't get it off!"

Brindle looked closely and saw what the problem was. There was a sticky piece of paper clinging to the bottom of her shoe. Brindle gently touched her horn to the paper and pulled it off from Hannah. The only problem now was that it was stuck to Brindle's horn!

"Oh, Brindle!" Hannah laughed and crawled out of her hidey-hole. She reached out and grabbed the piece of paper off of Brindle's horn. "Thank you, Brindle. I have missed you."

"I was just thinking about you, Hannah," Brindle said with a smile. "Here, let me make that go away with my magic."

"Silly," Hannah said. "That is a wonderful thing, but you don't have to be magic to take care of this."

Hannah took the piece of paper, crumpled it up and walked over to a garbage can on the playground and threw the paper in.

"You're right!" Brindle said. "You don't have to be magic to do that!"

Brindle looked around the playground, noticing the garbage all over the place. Pieces of paper, wrappers, plastic, and soda cans were crumpled all over, making the playground look not so fun after all.

"Is the trash the reason that kids don't come here to play anymore?" Brindle asked.

"I think so," Hannah said sadly. "I never see kids come here anymore."

"Then maybe we can clean this place up and children can come to find the magic here again!" Brindle offered.

"Really, Brindle?" Hannah asked. "That would be wonderful!"

"Then let's get started!" Brindle laughed.

She and Hannah spent the rest of the afternoon cleaning up all the mess on the playground that careless people had left behind. When they were done, Brindle and Hannah sat together on the merry-go-round, gently turning to see all of the cleaning they had done.

"It looks wonderful, Brindle!" Hannah said happily. "Thank you so much!"

"Of course, Hannah!" Brindle smiled. "I love to help my friends. And maybe now you can make some new friends."

Brindle pointed her horn to where some children were coming to look at the now clean playground.

"You go meet them and I will come by again and see you again someday."

"Thank you again, Brindle!" Hannah gave Brindle a quick hug and ran off to make some new friends with the children in her neighborhood.

Brindle smiled and left, but checked back every once and a while to watch the children play. It was the kind of magic that was better than any other... the magic of friendship and play!

Brindle and the Blue Unicorn

Brindle the magical white unicorn with a beautiful golden horn was out and about, walking around as she usually did when she was out for adventure when she noticed the sky was an interesting color.

"I wonder what color that is?" asked Brindle curiously.

Confused and staring at the sky, Brindle was at a loss.

"Excuse me," said a new unicorn Brindle had never met. "I see that you are staring at the sky."

Brindle looked down from the sky at this new friend.

"Oh my," thought Brindle. "This Unicorn is the same color as the sky. Maybe he can help me figure out what color the sky is. Maybe I should not ask him to help? It is not always easy to ask for help?"

"Hi," said Brindle. "I am looking at the sky and I see that it is the same color as you are. May I ask, what color are you?"

"Of course, I will tell you my color!" said the unicorn. "I am always happy to help and share, it makes me feel good to help others. I am the color Blue."

"Blue, huh?" said Brindle. "I am trying to learn what colors are because I think I like colors. You are my first color. It is nice to meet you, Blue Unicorn. Is that your name?"

"Yes, we all share the color names so that we can all be together. I love the color Blue, and I am very glad it is your first color that you have learned. There are many different colors and I can introduce you to them if you want." The Blue unicorn said.

"That would be wonderful!" said Brindle. "But I have more questions before we go to meet your friends. Like... what is the color blue?"

"That is my favorite question to answer!" said the Blue Unicorn. "Blue is one of three primary colors in painting and nature. With the science of nature, Blue lies between violet and green on the spectrum of light. Your eyes see blue when it is observing light between 450 and 495 nanometers."

"That is Blue," the Blue Unicorn said proudly. "What do you think about what I just said?"

"That is very confusing and complicated," said Brindle. "I am not sure I understand what you just said. I know! I can use my horn on you to see what blue is... maybe that will be easier."

"My horn makes things turn blue. What does your horn do?" asked the Blue Unicorn.

"It tells me what emotions are, among other things," said Brindle. "I like to ask permission before I use my horn on someone. May I try it on you?"

"Of course! Be my guest!" said the Blue Unicorn.

Brindle powered up her horn and began to see the color blue in connection with her new unicorn friend.

"It is interesting that most people associate sadness to the color Blue," said the Blue Unicorn. "That is not entirely true. I look forward to seeing what your horn sees."

Brindle relaxed and let the color blue swim around her. "Oh my, this is a very boy color. Boys normally are thought of as blue. And look... deep blue is a very powerful color when it comes to working. This color has much depth and stability. It is trusting with intelligence. Oh, I like this color!" said Brindle.

Then Brindle turned her horn on even more. Oh… light blue is the color of the sky, whereas dark blue makes you feel very serious thought. This is a very stable emotion I am feeling.

"Blue is a very wonderful color!" announced Brindle. "It is very intelligent and stable."

The Blue Unicorn puffed up his chest with pride and his horn glowed.

"Oh, thank you very much! That is very much how I feel. I am very proud to be stable and smart. Thank you, Brindle. You are my new friend and you make me feel good. I hope your horn can tell that I am very happy."

"It does!" Brindle smiled.

"Shall we meet my other friends of color? I am sure they will really like meeting you. And you can use your horn on all of them to see what they are like. This is very interesting... You are a very interesting unicorn, Brindle."

Brindle powered down her horn and smiled. She liked to make new friends... so how could she say no? Anyways, she really did not have much to do today other than learning and adventuring... and learning is the best.

"It would be my pleasure to meet your friends!" said Brindle.

"Then off we go! Follow me," the Blue Unicorn replied.

The Unicorn and the Eagle

Brindle was a very special unicorn. She was bright white with a beautiful glowing golden yellow horn. Brindle loved to make new friends and help people. Best of all, Brindle was a magical unicorn!

It was a bright sunny day, and Brindle was walking around, admiring the clouds as they floated across the sky, making shadows on the fields as she walked. It was a happy day!

One shadow moved faster than the others, and Brindle looked up to see a large, beautiful bird flying overhead, circling the spot where she stood in the field. When the bird saw her looking up, it made slow, sweeping circles downward, until it finally landed in the field in front of Brindle.

"Hello there!" The bird smiled at Brindle. "I am Elli the eagle. What is your name? And what kind of creature are you? I have never seen one of you before."

Brindle laughed. "Hi Elli, I am Brindle, and I'm a unicorn. A magic unicorn." She added.

"I have never seen a unicorn before!" Elli said excitedly. "I wonder why that is?"

"I don't know, "Brindle said. "Although there aren't that many of us unicorns around. I think that may have something to do with it."

"Maybe," Elli said. "Hey, Brindle... would you like to come flying with me? Unicorns can fly, right? But I thought they were supposed to have wings."

"You are thinking of a Pegasus," Brindle said. "A Pegasus has wings. Unicorns have horns."

"Oh," Elli said. "I was hoping for someone to play within the skies today. I guess I'll just have to keep looking."

Brindle could feel Elli's disappointment.

"Well..." said Brindle, trying to make Elli feel better. "I don't have wings, but I am magic. Maybe I can magic myself into being able to fly with you."

"Really?" Elli asked. "Can you really do that?"

"I don't know," Brindle admitted. "I have never tried. Let me see if I can."

Brindle focused hard on the magic in her horn. She tried to magic herself into flying. But it didn't work. She was disappointed. Worse yet, she could feel that Elli was again disappointed too.

"Oh, well," Elli said. "At least you tried."

"Well..." Brindle thought hard. "Maybe I can't fly that way. But maybe you can pick me up and carry me, and we can fly together!"

Elli looked at Brindle, judging her size. "I am a big bird, for sure. But I don't think that even I could carry a unicorn. You are just too big and heavy."

"My magic may not be able to help me fly," Brindle smiled. "But it can make me smaller!" And with just a thought, Brindle used the magic in her horn, and she started shrinking down to the size of a cat.

"Oh!" Elli said happily. "Now I can carry you!"

"We only have a little bit of time before it wears off," Brindle said. "So, we'd best get this adventure started!"

Elli happily jumped up into the air and then swooped down and picked Brindle up. Together they soared across the sunny sky. Brindle was excited to fly, and she and her new friend chatted happily until it was time to come down again.

The Unicorn and the Spider

Brindle was a beautiful, white magical unicorn with a golden horn. Brindle's favorite things in the whole world were to make new friends, learn new things, and to help people.

Brindle was walking through the woods one day when something dropped down on her nose. This startled Brindle, as she wasn't used to things dropping out of the sky and landing on her. She looked cross-eyed down her nose to see what it was, trying to focus in without shaking it off.

When she could finally focus, Brindle saw that it was a little brown creature that had landed on her nose and was now crawling around, tickling Brindle's nose. Brindle couldn't help it. She tried to stay still, but the tickling made her nose feel funny.

Prickling started inside her nose and suddenly, Brindle couldn't help it anymore. She sneezed.

"Achoo!"

The little creature hung on for dear life, staying stuck to Brindle's nose.

"Aren't you a spider?" Brindle finally was able to ask after she sneezed.

"Yes, I am," the little spider said proudly. "My name is Sadie."

"Hi, Sadie," Brindle said. "My name is Brindle. I have always been afraid of spiders. Right now, you don't seem so scary."

"I know," Sadie said with a touch of sadness. "Everyone seems to be afraid of spiders."

Brindle hated it when anyone felt sad, and she felt bad for Sadie. "I think it's because you look different from everyone else."

"Different how, do you think?" Sadie asked.

"Well..." Brindle thought about it for a minute. "You don't have eyes that are like everyone else's."

"My eyes are like everyone else's," Sadie said. "I use them to see. I have eight eyes instead of two. Some of them are because I am so little, that the extra eyes help me to see things move so that I can keep safe."

"I didn't know that," said Brindle. "But why do you have so many legs? That seems a little scary too."

"I have so many legs because I need them to help me to weave beautiful webs!" Sadie said with a smile. "Let me show you!"

Brindle watched while Sadie wove a beautiful web out of spider silk that came from out of her body. When she finished, Brindle looked at it very closely.

"That is very beautiful, Sadie!" Brindle said. "And I watched you while you were weaving. It really took a lot of work with those many legs of yours to make something so beautiful."

"Thank you, Brindle," Sadie said, blushing.

"No, thank you, Sadie," Brindle said. "Thank you for showing me something so beautiful when I was once afraid of spiders. Now I can see things in a much different way. Just because something or someone is different, it doesn't mean that they are scary. It means that they are special!"

"Do you really think that I'm special?" Sadie asked.

"Of course, you are!" Brindle said. "Can I add something to your web, so that I can be part of how special you are?"

"Oh!" Sadie said. "Of course!"

Brindle called the magic in her horn and then touched it to Sadie's web. Sparkles of magic came out of her horn and touched the web, making it shine and glitter in the sunlight.

"Oh, Brindle!" Sadie breathed happily. "You have made my web truly beautiful!"

"No," Brindle said. "I just helped make it so others could see it for how beautiful it already was."

"Well, thank you, Brindle," Sadie said sincerely. "Would you like to do some more with me?"

"I would love to!" Brindle laughed happily.

Sadie and Brindle spent the rest of the day together making beautiful, sparkling webs for everyone to see.

CONCLUSION

Congratulations on making it to the end. I hope my bedtime stories may have been to your child's liking and have given him a sweet dream. Which fairytale did he like the most? Whenever your child wants to hear a fantastic bedtime story, take this book and choose the one you prefer and let the imagination run wild.

CPSIA information can be obtained
at www.ICGtesting.com
Printed in the USA
BVHW090954030621
608731BV00011B/2217